AF578286

Middle Mississippians

University of Central Florida · Contemporary Poetry Series

MIDDLE MISSISSIPPIANS

Encounters with the Prehistoric Amerindians

Ted Hirschfield

University Press of Florida
Gainesville / Tallahassee / Tampa / Boca Raton
Pensacola / Orlando / Miami / Jacksonville

All photographs by Margaret Hirschfield

01 00 99 98 97 96 C 6 5 4 3 2 1

01 00 99 98 97 96 P 6 5 4 3 2 1

Library of Congress Cataloging-in-Publication Data
Hirschfield, Ted, 1941–
Middle Mississippians: encounters with the prehistoric Amerindians / Ted Hirschfield.
p. cm. — (Contemporary poetry series)
ISBN 0-8130-1399-2 (cloth). — ISBN 0-8130-1430-1 (pbk.)
1. Indians of North America—Antiquities—Poetry. 2. America—Discovery and exploration—Spanish—Poetry. 3. Soto, Hernando de, ca. 1500-1542—Poetry. 4. Mississippian culture—Poetry. I. Title. II. Series: Contemporary poetry series (Orlando, Fla.)
PS3558.I673M5 1996
811'.54—dc20 95-42860

The University Press of Florida is the scholarly publishing agency for the State University System of Florida, comprised of Florida A & M University, Florida Atlantic University, Florida International University, Florida State University, University of Central Florida, University of Florida, University of North Florida, University of South Florida, and University of West Florida.

University Press of Florida
15 Northwest 15th Street
Gainesville, FL 32611

For Tecumseh and Simon Kenton:
Americans

"Who Mourns for Logan?"

—CHIEF LOGAN

CONTENTS

HERNANDO DE SOTO

TENANT FARMERS

ACKNOWLEDGMENTS

Wilfred No Ear, wherever you are; Duane Randel, who knows what the wind says in Kansas; Louis D. Rubin, the last incarnation of H. L. Mencken; Robert W. Hamblin, who took *Human Weather* into his hands and saw it published; L. D. Brodsky, who commissioned *German Requiem* and gave me the courage to write it; Michael Waxenberg, a just man who loves freedom; and my wife, Margaret, who gives me birth after miraculous birth.

INTRODUCTION

The first time I climbed the steep slope of a temple mound thirty years ago, I found a complete pottery vessel near the level top, barely grazed by the plow which had tossed it out of the ground. It lay in a deep furrow between two rows of corn, washed clean by the rains, looking as though it was waiting to be put back on a shelf.

I think I stood there for a long time, breathing in the rich and living earth, almost afraid to touch it because I would be the first human to hold it in a thousand years. When I finally lifted the water bottle by its neck, I knew I had made contact with the unknown woman who had made it and the sense of communion that flowed through me has never left me.

Today the mound is gone, and one has to lie flat on the ground to see the small rise where it once stood. Many other wonderful things are gone, thanks to the ever-increasing efficiency of the farm machines that define our progress. As we belatedly try to make our peace with the past in resurrecting something of the spirit of the indigenous peoples of this continent, I hope this book may serve as a living memorial to a silenced people who have entered our cultural mainstream in ways we cannot even begin to imagine.

TRAVELOGUE

Self-Portrait Through a Windshield

One hand playing with the steering wheel,
He points, one finger punctuating time:
"They were there and there and over there."
And they appear along his extended arm,
Called up again to walk in single file,
The smoke haze rising from brushfires.
You can see them reflected in his eyes,
The pupils of his outer inner landscape.

"That low mound in the middle of the field?
Twenty years ago it was still covered up
With trees, looking like a natural hill.
Now you have to know it was there at all,
Almost gone in the geographic blender.
I think the farm plow is like democracy,
It levels everything into the ground."
Analogies move quickly with the car.

"See that creek line coming up ahead?
We'll be there in about thirty seconds.
It was a good place for a winter camp.
Look sharp, you'll see a deep worn trail
Going down to the edges of the water.
Should take a picture before it is gone.
A lot of Dover flint came out of there."
The image is gone at sixty miles an hour.

"And those are the Pine Hills on our left,
Crossing with the Mississippi up ahead.
It was a place where mastodon were trapped.

They've found wagonloads of mired bones.
Occasional Clovis points are also found
On the first terrace high above the river."

"To your right, along the riverbanks,
For years they've been quietly excavating,
I mean the National Geographic Society.
They found an actual Dalton site, in situ.
They were the best engineers in stone.
Those Dalton people loved their flint,
Chipped out a masterpiece in minutes."

"See the low bluffs rising on our left?
The small dark opening in the sandstone?
That's where their young men sat alone
Until they were starved into a vision.
A sun circle is carved into the ceiling.
I'll take you there sometime and show you."

"And now we come to my favorite story,
That ridge line cutting through the road.
Years ago, a farmer found an effigy pot
The mules kicked out beside the plow,
A small figure squatting on its haunches.
When the tenant farmer moved to Alabama,
A local collector followed him down there,
Years later, and brought it back to Illinois."

FIELD NOTES

Mississippian Petroglyphs, Fountain Bluff, Illinois

Once you see the opening of a trail
Cutting across the railroad tracks,
Park the car and get out slowly:
You are now approaching holy ground
Through canopies of overhanging trees,
Insidious patches of poison ivy
Climbing the last leg of the hill
And a heavier gravity of silence
Pulling down on the weight of time.

Catch your breath and there it is,
Suddenly, appearing all at once:
A rock wall broken from the mass
Of fallen boulders lying at its base,
A smooth-faced declivity in stone
Overgrown with moss and lichen,
The roof line covered up with soot,
The layered smoke of a thousand fires.

Stand there in the semidarkness.
Your eyes will focus into vision
Of living things along the wall:
A profusion of pictures cut in stone
Caught in the act of living motion,
Painted deep in reds and yellows,
Earth paints of red and yellow ocher,
The colors buried in flint nodules
Mixed with bear grease for a binder.

Collages of impossible birds
Commonly known as thunderbirds,
Turtles swimming seas of stone
And evidence of ancient terror:
A snake is swallowing the sun,
A solar eclipse in the making,
Darker than the mind which drew it
And repetitions of sun circles—
The emblem of their universe.

A deer was used for target practice,
Its body cavity scored with lead,
The pointillistic pattern of a .22
And complaints of adolescent love:
"Kriegie Loves - - -" all shot away.
The secular graffiti of the holy,
The obliviousness of the modern ego,
Of animals living in the present:
Kriegie probably is paying alimony.

And then there are the human hands:
Handprints carved into the solid rock,
The fingers spread in a wide display
To take the outline of the hand.
Stand on the boulder over there:
He was about your present height,
Your fingers find the hollow channels,
Superimposed in a perfect fit,
And tell me you don't feel anything.

A Spanish-Style Axe Found at Ware, Illinois

It was made in validation of a rumor
In remembered image of the original,
Traded overland or up the Mississippi,
In native copper from the Spanish steel.
It was probably encountered in Alabama
And found one day in a plowed-up field.
And rumor has me leaning on the case,
One of those dreary Victorian pieces,
A relic left from the pharmaceutical.
It's smaller than it looked at first,
Which makes it seem even more authentic:
The scale was drawn in the maker's mind.
(And objects behind glass seem larger
And they always look more valuable.)
It has part of the wooden handle left
Where it was protected by the metal.
In shape, it is more than reminiscence,
In the curving memory of scimitars,
The peaked edges of the Spanish mind.
The archeologists will never accept it;
It lacks the chosen place of provenance.
But imagination will always be truer
And you place it back into its case.

The Monster of Keokuk

She lifts him from the bottom shelf,
Moving aside the garage sale stuff:
Bric-a-brac in unknown destination,
Of leftover lives in sad mementos.

The Object

He is made of finely polished sandstone,
About fifteen inches high, when standing:
His body is rigid in suggesting death,
The hair is in a topknot to the left,
Two human head masks cover both ears
(They were undoubtedly made of shell).
One hand is holding a sacrificial knife,
A curved flint mace, flat on his chest,
And on his right side, when turning him:
A severed head is hanging from his hand.

Provenance

His father found it doing road work
Somewhere once in southern Illinois.
How long ago can only be your guess.
The folded sheet of dog-eared paper,
Barely literate and sealed in grease,
A typewritten sheet in hunt and peck
Has traveled the better side of time.
In turning it over you draw a blank,
Hold it to the light for validation
And end up falling back on intuition.

Authenticity

The cultural index of the artifact
Is accurately Middle Mississippian:
The head and masks are in triangles,
The weeping eye in wavering lines,
The hair style is especially striking,
Combining individual style and fashion.
Metal tools do not have the patience
Of fits and starts in the broken lines.
The minor breakage is all healed over
To the same patina of the overall whole.

Summary

Everything is right except the eyes.
What they see will never be described.
They are the encircled eyes of horror,
Accented in the round and opened wide.
They lack serenity, the Oriental slant:
The alive-in-death look of the East,
Surprisingly like white men's eyes,
Our eyes that cannot see through time.
They are Western and too metaphysical
In reflecting his own inner blindness.

Surface Hunters

In better times they were eccentrics,
Antiquarians and generally respected
For being different without a fault.
Today they are considered antisocial
For being sane and self-contained,
Mislabeled for preferring solitude.
Some you only know by distant rumor
And ten rows over in an open field,
Walking away in opposite directions.
Others are self-discovered alcoholics,
Walking off their penance to the past:
All who are born out of their time
Or simply trading their addictions
Dead at the center of their visions.

All looking for something tangible,
Walking between the seams of time,
Humping the chasms of the present.
Anything made by the hand of man.

Bending over, touch and pick it up.
It's better than a human handshake.
Ending up in personal possession
And good enough to last a lifetime,
A living communion with the dead:
Loudest affirmation of the present.

The Open Field

I.

The magic of mornings in an open field:
Late fall and early spring are always best
When fields are vacant between cultivation.
Your feet pick up the rhythm of the earth,
Following the furrows until they converge
In stereoscopic vision measuring distance.
The eyes are trained like hunting dogs,
Channel-surfing a wide expanse of sight,
Eyes nervously on edge for the unusual,
Skimming the furrows from side to side,
Every found piece of litter and debris,
Anything that shows up in geometric form
To suggest it has been touched by man.

Flint flakes every color of the rainbow,
Washed clean from the surrounding soil,
Pottery shards soaked through by the rains
Almost look like they are brand new again,
Cannel coal is blacker than the earth,
Pipestone is deep red or in a banded grey,
Paintstones are mostly in reds or yellows
And sometimes white in a graphic contrast,
Small squares of heavy worked galena lead
That momentarily trick the weighing hand,
The dark green or black of polished celts,
The shimmer of faceted fluorspar jewelry
Catches the sun ten feet ahead of you
And fragments of copper in brightest green
Among the dark translucence of obsidian.

II.

Another hot day in August, late in the month,
Locked in by air-conditioning all summer long:
At six a.m., the temperature is already ninety.
The weather front is stalled above your house,
Afternoons are threatening showers every day
In parting cloud farts of undigested rumblings
And inside the house you are now going crazy,
Reading too much and looking out the window,
Your energy sapped, used by your imagination.
And every night you dream of the open fields,
The mother of all fields in perfect artifacts,
A field strewn thicker with litter and debris
Where all the objects seem to be personified,
A wide expanse of open fields in Vistavision,
With all the relics enhanced in living color.

And one fine morning, to your own surprise,
You stumble up from the right side of the bed,
Throw on a quick and minimal cover of clothing
And drive like hell out to your favorite site,
Running through the high grass, down the levee,
Flushing a frightened black snake at the bottom
And reaching the lined-up rows of wilting corn,
A tall forest of corn seared badly by the heat
And take a quick and first look at the ground
And there it is, right there in front of you,
Only two inches away from your sandaled foot:
A white and round and perfect fluorspar pendant
And almost without stopping, you scoop it up
And turn and run like hell back to your car.

Ode to the Dalton Projectile Point

What we know about them can be summarized,
All too briefly, in journals of the trade:
Hunter-gatherers with the built-in instinct
To keep forever moving, following the game
And tending to stay in dark rock shelters.
They kept to themselves on the high ridges
Above the sloughs and swamps, on their bluffs:
Forty feet down in professional excavations.

All too briefly, without a known language,
The unrecorded laughter of their children,
Their skeletal remains are more than scarce.
Yet what they left is nothing but astonishing,
The final keepers of a fluted, long tradition
And past masters in the art of shaping stone:
The paleorocket scientists of projectile points.

At once more sensitive to experimentation
Than their forefathers, the Clovis people,
With more imagination than the Folsom point
And selective in their choice of finest flint.

Twisting the hard stone to level it in flight,
They mastered the first secrets of ballistics:
The flakes run in rippled motions to the edges
Like water quick-frozen in the act of motion
To the graceful curvature of its arching base,
And left a mystery in their red-tipped points
As if they had applied a final touch of paint
Until you see the coloration is in the stone.

You have to carry and handle one for hours,
Absentmindedly turning it over in your hand
While you are doing something entirely else,
A better worry stone for your preoccupations
When you are making out your monthly bills;
And it will come alive within your grasp:
The point of your life and its sharp edges,
The base which you made smooth and safer,
The outward curve of your sharp ambitions
With a hardened ridge right at the center:
Your target made visible in your sure aim.

TEMPLE MOUNDS

Temple Mound, Reynoldsville, Illinois

Thirty years ago, it was three times as high,
The approach ramp visible in gradual incline
Climbing up to the very threshold of the sky
In its gently squared and angled definitions.
Now it is roundcd away and down by plowing,
The platform of the sun reclining to the earth,
Surrendering to earth and force of gravity,
Forced down and outward by the bitten plow
In traded ecologies of time in fair exchange:
The harrowed earth is slowly turning over,
Upward direction lost in pointing to the east.

There should be something at the center,
Probably at ground level, in the center,
If you can find the center of a level field.
The plow will reach it in its unhurried time
And toss the bones out to the bleaching sun—
The walk now is easier to the leveled top.

The wind you felt here thirty years ago,
The hunger sharp and grabbing at your throat
Has settled to a gentled horizontal flow
Like everything else plowed down around you.
Reclaiming half an acre for a bumper crop,
The wind and earth and sun plowed down,
The sharp edges gone and undifferentiated
In the widening expanses of a leveled field.

The Great Temple Mound, Cahokia, Illinois

In area, it is larger than the pyramids of Egypt,
In effort, greater than the cathedrals of Europe:
An average basket of earth weighed eighteen pounds,
Multiplied by how many millions on their backs?
How many centuries did they carry on their backs?
It was built as a timeless tribute to the earth,
From earth, and a resting place for the living sun,
A stepping-stone placed in the middle of creation.
Aesthetically, it looms as rival to small mountains
But carefully separated from the rest of nature,
To make it plain: This is the handiwork of man.
And what it has survived is even more impossible:
The Trappist Brothers borrowed it for a retreat,
Using it as a footstool for their silenced god,
Plain as the great church topping great Cholula:
Ironic churches sentenced to an exclamation point,
The foundations of the church and mound are pagan.
Popularly it is still referred to as "Monk's Mound."
The Brothers farmed the leveled top in vegetables—
Once more they are in retreat from their own age.
It is yearly climbed by hordes of modern Boy Scouts
With weary senior citizens milling around its base.
Bordered close by the oblivious expressway traffic,
It is a constant reminder they are going nowhere
In closed air-conditioned cars and blasting stereos.
It has a modern visitor's center: every visual aid
To help the American Indians make themselves at home.

Temple Mound, Cape Girardeau, Missouri

It lies behind the industrial park,
The sacred precincts of our progress,
Half sheared away in mutilated form
By some Jaycee booster's wet dream
Spawned in a nearby local restaurant
And sanctioned by the city fathers.

Gone bust and belly-up and bankrupt,
Crowded together with tract houses,
The future is parceled out in lots
Too small for life, too practical,
To outlast built-in obsolescence.

A few million basketloads of earth
Carried here for a hundred years,
Divided up by the foot and dollar
And bulldozed down by a Caterpillar?

Without a signal marker or a sign
And fences are not cost-effective.
To leave it standing as a local park
Would mean the cost of maintenance,
The cost of leaving anything alone.

Kincaid Mounds, Olmsted, Illinois

I suggest you take a little trip
With your family and your friends.
Call it "A Trip to Yesteryear"
Or something equally edifying.
Plan the weekend in advance,
"A family weekend expedition,"
An hour from the Ramada Inn.
Adopt your "touristy" attitude,
Pack in an extra little lunch
On the light side of cholesterol
Or just buy it from the Colonel.
A designer double roll of Bounty.
Put the emphasis back in "fun"
For deficit children of attention.
Bring along a can of insect spray
And check the air-conditioning.
Take along a box of Glad or Hefty
For your family and your friends.

You should never go alone to Kincaid.
It's off the beaten track by centuries
And you might get lost in finding it.
Actually, it's not that hard to find
If you learn to leave yourself behind.

Stand there in the middle of the plaza.
Someone will come up quietly beside you
And call you out by a different name.
You can blame the voices on the crows
Flying from mound to mound above you.

Someone will touch you on the shoulder.
Turn around, and you'll see yourself:
A faceless man, stripped to the skin,
Someone you think you should have known,
Holding two rattles in his clenched hands.

Even if you can make it back alive,
Your car will look monstrous, alien.
And praying for the first paved road,
You cannot shake the dust behind you,
A feeling you did not bring with you.

Temple Mound, Ware, Illinois

I.

Among all mounds, she was my favorite,
The most generous in giving artifacts.
The price she exacted was the intimate
(Her teaching style was the confessional).
The surrender of what should be hidden,
And who in wearing away is always giving
More than what she was given in return.
Her name is spelled out in civilization.
She outlasted her ownerships and changes
And taught me how to walk back in time.

One year, along her gentle terraces,
She gave up her inventories of bone:
Deer ulna awls that fit in the thumb,
Small, sharp needles from bird bone,
Polished counters used for gambling
To keep the men well inside the home;
A hollowed-out piece of grinding stone.

She remained suspended in revelation,
Between fascination and the awesome.
The massive birth she always promised,
Sometimes almost edged raw with fear,
She gives up in random playfulness:
Children's toys drawn from the clay,
Her thumbprint is on a little rattle,
Marbles rolled between her fingers,

A ceramic disc to teach her children
The four true directions of the earth,
The drawn map of the world around her.

II.

Walking for hours in a hypnotic state
You are one with the place you walk,
One day torn from the calendar of March,
Your shoulders hunched against the wind,
Raw fingers thrust deep in your pockets.
And standing alone on the temple mound
Before deciding to walk back to the car,
She revealed herself to you at last
In grace and epiphany of the moment:
The sun broke through among the clouds
And walked across the fields below
Until it reached your stopping point.
And there, in one long shaft of light,
You saw the outline of their houses:
Small squares, darker than the soil,
The house sites all appearing in a row
With narrow walkways in between them.
The sunlight slanted down just once;
Then it was gone and closed up again.
The fields seemed darker than before
As the wind drove ice into your face
And you slowly walked back to your car.

III.

She must have been old and heavy-boned,
Her skeleton lay in full articulation,
Washed into being by new spring rains
Between two mounds on a gradual slope
With her sewing kit laid out beside her:
Two long needles made from turkey bone,
The original bone replaced by minerals
Made shinier by her constant weaving
And shuttling of the long-stemmed grass.
A spindle whorl lay near her pelvis,
A small, round disk of granular sandstone
Worn smooth about six hundred years ago
And also several of her shorter needles:
Fine-pointed to their business ends,
Still sharp enough to prick the skin.
A line of demarcation in the ground
And subtle evidence of discoloration
Showed where her leather bag had been.
She lay just inches under the plow line
And waiting for the new spring rains
To bring her back into her life again.

IV.

Digging at the base of the smaller mound
With only several hours of daylight left,
He says there must be intrusive burials
In there somewhere and added much later,
Probably by people of a related culture
Who liked this strangely unremembered place
As a ready-made site to bring their dead.
He handles the hand spade like a surgeon,

Separating the earth in clean-cut sheets
And stops short at the sound of scraping—
A line of white appearing just below him:
The sound and sight of uncovered bone.
Soon he is lifting out the whole skull
And goes on looking for the missing body
And comes up lifting out another skull
And then another and more, another one,
Until thirteen skulls are looking at us.
Thirteen skulls placed in a full circle
And the night is falling fast around us
And nothing else was buried with them.
"Probably sacrificial," he is muttering,
"Damned trophy heads for a dedication."
And quickly he covers them all up again.
Carefully he covers them up with earth
While the night is falling all around us.

HERNANDO DE SOTO

Inquisition

Adelantado:
Which was heavier?
The cross or the gold
You never found?

The Lament of Tuscaloosa

When they came into our country,
At first, the people were afraid,
Saying that these were all the sons
Of the Great Serpent, hearing them
Coming before we could see them:
They were talking in loud voices
With a noise like bluejays make,
Beating down the narrow game trails
As they came through the canebrakes
And they owned everything they saw.

Some were riding on a strange deer
As if they were one larger animal
And we saw them stop and separate
Until they became two animals again.
They were hairy all over like bears
And had unsightly hair on their faces,
Talking through their hairy anus faces
And had long dirty hair on their heads
Like the color of our ripening corn
And some, the color of bright copper.

They carried a strong smell with them
That offended us, especially the deer
Which sweated white froth in their mouths.
We watched the men-like beings defecate
And examined their droppings in secret
And they looked and smelled like ours.
Their headdresses shaped like the moon,
Their bodies had a hard metal clothing

That looked like long sheets of mica;
At first we thought it was their skin.

They had weapons made of the same metal:
They carried long and narrow war clubs
Which were wrapped in leather pouches,
Some were shorter and some were longer.
They were sharper than our flint knives
And aimed them at our heads and arms.
And the more we managed to wound them
The more they kept coming on in groups,
Shouting what sounded like their singing,
The large deer with angry rolling eyes.

The strangers are not civilized like us
With rude, round eyes like discoidals:
They do not seem to be one common people
And do not make war with any ceremony.
They have no fear of the dead; their own
Dead they quickly hide away in the earth.
We did not see them talking to the dead
And when we took them out of the ground
To hang up as offerings in our temples,
They were as white as the color of death.

They never saw us, even when up close,
Even when they walked right among us:
Up the stairs of the great temple mound,
Laying their rough hands on the priests,
Breaking open the boxes of our caciques

And kicking their bones out of place.
When they left us they took everything:
All our beans and our corn and squashes.
We knew we had seen something strange
No one had ever told us about before.

Temple Mound, Memphis, Tennessee

When de Soto rode his horses to the top
Of the mounds at Chucalissa on the bluffs,
Looking westward in long Spanish miles,
The endless miasmal swamps beneath him,
He did not know that his horse's hooves
Had already killed the power in that place.

The temples were polluted by his presence:
The impatient horses pawing at the ground
Had driven out the mana stored up there.
The living ancestors buried in that place,
Who were collected in the layered mounds,
Charged the earth with their sacred being.

De Soto turned to ride reluctantly away,
Carrying dreams in empty Spanish pockets.
Sacrifices would follow him with curses,
The dead were heard shouting in their sleep,
The blood would flow down from the temples:
Torrents of blood to drown out his memory.

The Relation of de Soto

When I shall return to Extremadura,
God willing, I will tell the Virgin
Of Guadalupe of this cursed place
And seek remission, but not for the
Savages, the servants of the devil.
Besides, they make poor servants
And run away after they mislead us.
A pestilence of insects larger than
A Moor's head, the tangled swamps
And vines tripping up the horses.
We lose all our sense of direction
And go in circles until we strike
The rivers which seem always dark
And steep and all looking the same.
We are reduced to eating the maize
For horses; the little holy wine—
The priests keep it for themselves.
I would give much for honest bread.
The leather rots in this foul heat,
Not to mention what it does to steel,
Good Toledo steel rusts in this place,
And the horses suffer, always wounded.
Our own breathing is made very heavy
Like drinking water in this wet heat
And yet we are thirsty all the time.
I especially pray for the horses,
The savages aim at their bellies
And set ambushes and then fly away.
Naturales are afraid of the horses,
As we found true in Mexico and Peru.

The men will endure anything by far,
The nerve and patience of Castile.
Besides, they have nothing to lose
Being the aborted sons of poverty.
There are no open places anywhere
In this green hell of strange trees,
Not like the clean oaks of Extremadura.

In my Relation, I will not mention
I would rather die fighting the Moor
In Africa, if it please Our Majesty,
Than come back with more of nothing
From this place which offers nothing:
Gold that turns out to be copper,
Small bits of silver without a mine.
They do have freshwater pearls
Which they stupidly burn and bury
With their dessicated dead and keep
In wooden chests in their temples
And therefore are made worthless,
These blind servants of the serpent.
A poor place to die among heathen,
The savages are learning we can die.
They are losing their fear of the horses.

Whereas the Conquistadors Describe the Mounds

The Spanish did not see them
For what they were: after all,
They had been to Tenochtitlán,
A white-faced city in stone,
And fought the megalithic walls
Of far Cuzco in fabulous Peru.

"At the other side of the town
Was the temple, and on its top,
A wooden bird with gold eyes."
A comment like a tossed aside:
The eyes were inlaid copper
And already turning into gold.

A few middling mounds of earth:
Imagine, made of common earth,
Did not hold their interest.
They saw them "as theatres
And stages" for the caciques,
"With rough stairs going up."

"The cacique was on a balcony
That was made on a mound
To one side of the plaza."
Stages set for Spanish drama.
Now the mounds were balconies
Where chiefs were being fanned.

Simple men, these oaks of Spain,
Nor were they anthropologists

Trained to a fine disinterest:
"Entering the temple or oratory
Of these idolatrous people, we
Found bodies covered with pearls."

"With its authoritative oratory
On a high mound, the caney
Or houses of the caciques,
Very large and very tall
And broad, all covered, high
And lined with beautiful mats."

"They brought out from there
Eight or nine arrobas of pearls
And were very delighted."
The caciques took their cue
In order to get rid of them:
"Do you think this is a lot?"

"Go to Talimeco, my town,
And you will find so many
That you will be unable
To carry them on your horses."
But they could not find the town
Of the Lord, or any Indians.

Epitaph

De Soto lies buried in the Mississippi,
The perfect symbol for his wanderings.

His bones stuck in a low embankment,
Catfish and gar have picked him clean.

All his *Te Deums* did not save him
Without the absolution of a blessing.

Entradas that were merely incursions,
He made the sign of the cross in gold.

His brief epitaph lives on within us,
A people given to relentless change.

The river flows into our definitions,
Cutting new channels through his grave.

After de Soto

When Marquette and Joliet came in 1673,
Out of the wide mouth of the Wisconsin,
Accompanied by their few Illini guides,
Floating free in an eternity of water—
The Michisippi, almost an anonymous name,
"Big River" described in understatement,
They made their landfall on the Iowa side
And soon remarked upon the unremarkable:
The people were very proper and receptive
And let the Black Robes plant their cross.
Today there are left two low-lying mounds,
A few picnic tables, johnnies-on-the-spot,
A weatherbeaten sign that they were here
To help you to forget yourself in time.

Next they saw the Piasa Bird in Illinois,
A clawed monster painted on the bluffs,
An advertising sign for early travelers.
Their guides were frantic in their terror,
A simple Rorschach test for their religion
And showered their arrows through its body.
Later it was blasted away with dynamite.
At Tower Rock their guides deserted them:
The water swirled around a fearful suck,
Moaning sounds came from the whirlpool
And the Illiniwek went back to Illinois.
It was later blasted into our submission.

(One hundred–plus years since de Soto
And everything he had seen was gone

To be argued endlessly by archaeologists
In theories weighing less than paper:
Reams on the collapse of civilization,
Rampant diseases from the common cold,
Dead priests in democratic insurrections,
As if history waited for the historians
And books were equal to a living moment.)

At Cahokia the waterway was now open
And deserted: fifty-foot-long dugouts
Would otherwise have blocked their way
And netted them into its tributaries.
All the cities strung like river pearls
From far Aztalan to the Gulf of Mexico
Lay covered up with trees and grasses
Thick as memory, buried in their path:
Kincaid and Tula, Ware and Chucalissa.
Only the proud Natchez remained alive
Keeping the Great Sun in their temples,
A pitiful outpost of entropic empire
And soon enough they, too, would die,
Exterminated wholesale by the French.

A few escaped out to the high plains,
Scattered out in their transfixed fears,
Taking their rituals in diminished form
Out to a windswept and treeless place,
Where they would raise their world pole
Planted deep in the navel of the earth
And danced their remembered wanderings:
The Pawnee and Mandan and the Omahas
Built their houses in the shape of mounds
And moved inside the places of the dead.

Great temples became the medicine lodge
And the sun would now have to be carried
On their scalp hoops stretching over skin.
The dripping human heads became too heavy
For nomads in movement with a moving sun,
The sun that once was summoned from the top
Of the world each day by chanting priests.

TENANT FARMERS

Tenant Farmer, 1965

Stones rattling the undercarriage,
The car keeps to the center hump,
Riding the ruts on a leaning slant:
The dirt road running with the corn,
The fields, one long extended blur
Ending up in a wide expanse of yard
Littered with rusted-out machinery,
Locked in by weeds and castoffs left
By earlier tenants in their flight.
The farm dogs run in accompaniment
On the last dogleg into the yard
(They're earning their symbolic keep),
Chasing the wheels for fifty yards.

The house looks curiously unowned
Like all tenant houses everywhere,
No small patches of flowers anywhere
Or the suggestion of the feminine,
The seals of acceptance of a house.
The car stops with the motor running:
Get out with slow deliberate motion,
A part of the new surrounding scene,
Read the body language of the dogs,
Then walk toward the leaning gate,
Fenceposts topped by pieces of flint,
Flat pieces of broken Mill Creek flint
Large enough to notice from the tractor;
And now you know he's partially aware
Of what he's got growing in his fields.

You unlatch the gate unhurriedly
And follow the first law of the farm:
Always shut the gates behind you.
The screened-in porch is bulging out
And sagging down the falling stairs.
Then give them time to notice you,
Look around slowly at the ground
And hear a door shut from inside,
Time yet to look out at the fields
And he is coming up behind you:
A man held up by his suspenders,
His gut turned outward like a weapon,
His face a deeply cultivated field,
The image left fallow all the same.

One arm raised and quickly dropped,
He then eyes you over all at once
And knows you don't belong there:
You talk about the standing corn
Without a weed between the rows,
The weather looks like it will hold,
What is in crop and what is not,
The price of fertilizer is going up,
Farming the thin edges of disaster
And never adding up the final cost,
But somebody has to do it anyway,
The losing battle of all farming
Against the whims of far-off cities.
He thinks of moving into town soon,
His wife is working there part time,
His boy is going to technical school.

He slowly edges over to the fence,
(He finally knows why you are here)

Picks up a piece of dull, grey flint,
The polished bit of a broken hoe:
The break is old, almost healed over
To the natural color of the flint.
"The fields are full of it," he says.
Just last year when he plowed deeper
The stuff just kept on coming up in
Freeze and thaws, just keeps rising
And gets caught up in his machinery,
Tougher than roots of Johnson grass,
Just coming up from out of nowhere.

With small talk coming to an end,
You casually ask him if you can
(And turning slowly toward the car)
Walk his fields to look around?
The arrival at the moment of impasse.
He guesses not, the winter wheat
Is in and only now just coming up,
He's caught some people sneaking in
And leaving potholes in the fields,
He's even heard of Indians coming by
And digging in the mound for gold
And usually it is done at night.
"You can't trust people nowadays,
They've been hunting out of season,
One hunter even shot a cow last year,
Those weekend hunters from Chicago."

Still slowly walking to the car,
Making an exaggerated ceremony
Of opening and closing of the gate,
And now you are betting on the car

And hope his hearing is still good,
All the while with the motor running.

He cocks his head with a sudden grin,
Giving up to his sense of disbelief:
"You got a diesel motor in that car?
Imagine a diesel engine in a motor car!
Well, if that don't beat all."
He calls out to the waiting car:
"I guess it wouldn't hurt that much.
I guess you can come back sometime.
Just keep careful between the rows,
Don't be walking in the winter wheat.
You can come back almost anytime."

Honor Bound

He tells me there is a tenant farmer
Down near Vanduser, in the Bootheel,
Who has hit the mother lode, all right:
Hundreds of effigy vessels from a mound,
Human effigies, frog and opossum pots
And you wait till next Sunday afternoon
And make a beeline for the Hancock farms
While rehearsing every possible scenario,
Counting out your money ten times over
And snap the rubber band around the wad.

Cash in small bills talks the loudest,
Will have the last word of every deal:
Just peel off the bills into your hand
And keep it hanging out in open sight.
Make sure he sees the money all the time.
How much does a tenant farmer make?
There are no gentlemen farmers left.

You pass the house twice without notice,
Driving a perfect square of the six-forty,
Then riding back through your own dust
You pull up right smack outside the door:
A shotgun shack that looks deserted, grey,
A '51 Ford pickup under a shade tree,
The color worn off down to the primer
Or maybe it's just the even-colored rust.

You pull up right outside the door
Which opens when you reach for it:

He's nondescript and smiling at you,
He's seen you pass the house twice over
And you are down one at the beginning.

Then step into the house and stop
And feel the dirt floor under you.
Two little girls emerge from somewhere,
Their dresses made from flour sacks,
Their bare feet padding on the floor.
It's a picture from out of circa 1850,
A faded tintype, impossible for 1968.

And all along one wall of the shack,
He's found old bricks and boards,
Makeshift shelves, and row on row:
Dark pottery vessels from the earth,
The color drained up from the soil,
Two human head pots, side by side,
One human man pot, rarest of the rare,
Two painted vessels with sun circles,
More effigies than water bottles,
A real museum in being, uncataloged.

Unsnap the rubber band from the wad,
Start peeling bills into your hand
(The children study them wide-eyed,
A round woman filling in the doorway
Looking to the kitchen in the back),
And he's telling about who's been here,
Come to see him: State archaeologists,
Collectors, surface hunters, dealers,
And he won't sell any of it as yet—
He won't sell any of it ever, never.

You almost toss the wad of bills,
Look to the children for their help,
The closed-mouth woman in the back,
The woman fear-frozen into salt,
The smell of poverty all around.

Later, driving home on empty
And wearing off the double shock,
You finally figure it all out:
No one has ever come to see him.
No one has asked him for anything.
It has nothing to do with money.
He's found himself a sense of honor
And no one can take it away from him.

Red Barn

I.

Going out of town and south on Old 61,
El Camino Real, the highway of the king,
Was one of the few Hopewell sites left
In the whole real estate of Missouri:
A conical mound abutting the earthworks
Curving away from a large borrow pit
Where they took earth to raise the mound—
Now a stagnant pool of standing water,
A mosquito-expanding breeding ground.

And of all people, who should own it?
One good and credulous old Catholic,
Housebroken long ago by habituated ritual:
He knows the king's gold is buried there
And won't let anyone dig in the mound.
And no, he is not interested in old bones:
The Indians should await the resurrection,
Undisturbed and sitting on all that gold.
"Hell no," he won't sell it to the college:
"Education is a piece of paper and wasted
Time designed to turn out only soft-butts."
(You really can't argue with him there.)
He's seen what schools do with his money
And it hasn't done him one bit of good.

II.

The old man collected the eclectic
With a pack rat instinct carried over

From the hunger of the Great Depression.
He specialized in everything of the farm,
Uncommon common artifacts of agriculture
Caught right at the turning point of time
And already sanctified by false nostalgia.
Icons valued without the ground-in sweat:
Hames for horses and bits and spurs,
Milk cans, curry brushes, candle molds,
A pair of lost and lonely steer horns,
Wooden ox yokes inset with blank mirrors,
Four split and dehydrated wagon wheels,
Hall trees waiting for new wardrobes,
Worn-out chairs that keep the shape
Of former owners rocking in a corner,
Felt slouch hats that covered dim IQ's,
Misfiring spark plugs by the hundreds,
Guns that could shoot around a corner,
Short pieces of rotten, useless rope,
Coiled strands of rusted-out barbed wire:
The inventories of dead and dying farms,
Whole pickup loads of junk hauled home
From every auction around the county.

III.

Real nemesis came a few years later,
Too late, one cruel day in early June
And coming home from the Southwest,
Following in the wake of a tornado
Through avenues of slaughtered trees:

You turned off north, right onto 61
And felt it cold in your roiling gut,
(You feel it first before you see it)
And jerking the car into a tight U-turn,
Backtracking to your point of fear:
The clawed earth bare in desolation,
The mound is absolutely, finally, gone,
Hung with a For Sale sign for industry
And a Caterpillar sitting on a hill—
The mound is leveled to ground level.
You sensed a sudden clutch of paranoia:
The bastards waited till you were gone,
The old man dead to his own surprise
And attending the auction of his soul
And his heirs have not wasted any time.
There is no outrage in the local paper,
Not a sound of protest from the college.

What they left standing is the barn,
Home once of the Red Barn Burger,
A succession of failed enterprises:
An outlet for some mismatched shoes,
Then a craft shop for inspired boredom,
For love of frills and lace and bows—
Dressed and undressed dolls and doilies
Born in empty and middle-aged wombs.
And right behind it is the borrow pit,
The standing water turned to swamp:
It would cost too much to fill it in.

ABOUT THE AUTHOR

Margaret Hirschfeld

Theodore (Ted) Hirschfield was born Helmut Hirschfeld in Prussia, Germany, in 1941. During World War II, his father, a Baptist minister, was ousted from the pulpit and his family separated by the Nazis. Reunited in 1946, they emigrated to the United States in 1951.

Professor Hirschfield was educated at Ottawa University, Hollins College, Southern Illinois University, and Vanderbilt University. Since 1965, he has taught at Southeast Missouri State University in the Department of English.

A volume of his selected verse titled *Human Weather* appeared in 1991, followed by *German Requiem* in 1993. His poetry has been published in *The Cape Rock, Today, The Hollins Critic,* and *Arete: The Journal of Sport Literature.*

Mr. Hirschfield retired in 1995 and resides with his wife, Margaret, in Lehigh Acres, Florida.

University of Central Florida
Contemporary Poetry Series

Diane Averill, *Branches Doubled Over with Fruit*
George Bogin, *In a Surf of Strangers*
Van K. Brock, *The Hard Essential Landscape*
Jean Burden, *Taking Light from Each Other*
Lynn Butler, *Planting the Voice*
Daryl Ngee Chinn, *Soft Parts of the Back*
Robert Cooperman, *In the Household of Percy Bysshe Shelley*
Rebecca McClanahan Devet, *Mother Tongue*
Rebecca McClanahan Devet, *Mrs. Houdini*
Gerald Duff, *Calling Collect*
Malcolm Glass, *Bone Love*
Barbara L. Greenberg, *The Never-Not Sonnets*
Susan Hartman, *Dumb Show*
Lola Haskins, *Forty-four Ambitions for the Piano*
Lola Haskins, *Planting the Children*
William Hathaway, *Churlsgrace*
William Hathaway, *Looking into the Heart of Light*
Michael Hettich, *A Small Boat*
Ted Hirschfield, *Middle Mississippians*
Roald Hoffmann, *Gaps and Verges*
Roald Hoffmann, *The Metamict State*
Greg Johnson, *Aid and Comfort*
Markham Johnson, *Collecting the Light*
Hannah Kahn, *Time, Wait*
Michael McFee, *Plain Air*
Richard Michelson, *Tap Dancing for the Relatives*
Judith Minty, *Dancing the Fault*
David Posner, *The Sandpipers*
Nicholas Rinaldi, *We Have Lost Our Fathers*
CarolAnn Russell, *The Red Envelope*
Robert Siegel, *In a Pig's Eye*
Edmund Skellings, *Face Value*
Edmund Skellings, *Heart Attacks*
Floyd Skloot, *Music Appreciation*
Ron Smith, *Running Again in Hollywood Cemetery*
Katherine Soniat, *Cracking Eggs*
Don Stap, *Letter at the End of Winter*
Rawdon Tomlinson, *Deep Red*
Irene Willis, *They Tell Me You Danced*
John Woods, *Black Marigolds*